Prayers and Devotions for Teachers

With Contributions from Teachers, Pastors, and Christian Educators

Martha Whitmore Hickman

Abingdon Press / Nashville

Prayers and Devotions for Teachers

Copyright © 1989 by Abingdon Press

Third Printing 1992

This book is printed on recycled, acid-free paper.

Library of Congress Cataloging-in-Publication Data

HICKMAN, MARTHA WHITMORE
  Prayers and devotions for teachers.
  1. Sunday-school teachers—Prayer-books and devotions—English.
  I. Title.
  BV4596.S9H53 1989 242'.68 88-8188
  ISBN 0-687-33631-7 (pbk. : alk. paper)

Excerpts from *The Way of the Heart* by Henri J. M. Nouwen, Copyright
© 1981 by Henri J.M. Nouwen, are reprinted by permission of Harper
& Row, Publishers, Inc.

Scripture quotations noted RSV are from the Revised Standard Version
of the Bible, Copyright 1946, 1952, 1971 by the Division of Christian
Education of the National Council of Churches of Christ in the USA.
Used by permission.

Those noted GNB are from the Good News Bible, the Bible in Today's
English Version—Old Testament: Copyright © American Bible Society
1976; New Testament: Copyright © American Bible Society 1966, 1971,
1976. Used by permission.

Those noted JB are from The Jerusalem Bible, Copyright © 1966 by
Darton, Longman & Todd, Ltd. and Doubleday & Co., Inc. Used by
permission of the publishers.

Those noted NEB are from The New English Bible. © The Delegates of
the Oxford University Press and The Syndics of the Cambridge University Press 1961, 1970. Reprinted by permission.

Those noted KJV are from the King James Version of the Bible.

VENTURA® DESIGN BY JOHN R. ROBINSON

MANUFACTURED IN THE UNITED STATES OF AMERICA

CONTENTS

It's nine o'clock Saturday night in Anytown.

~ ~ ~

Margaret Allen sits at the dining room table. She runs her finger down the fold of her lesson book, flattening the pages, checks once more on the Bible passages, finds the construction-paper turkey made by drawing around your hand.

Her husband calls from the next room, "Don't you want to come watch the show?"

"In a minute," she answers. "I'm going over my lesson one more time."

~ ~ ~

At the university student center, Josh Morgan is talking with students. He stands.

"Gotta go," he says. "I want to check something for the Sunday school lesson. I hope I'll see some of you tomorrow."

~ ~ ~

In his favorite living room chair, Dr. B. R. Kenner reads through the lesson. He pauses, pushes his glasses back up on his nose and says to his wife, Marie, who is writing to their daughter in England, "Wouldn't you think they'd be tired of me after twenty years?"

~ ~ ~

They are teachers—Sunday school teachers. Josh also teaches biology at the university, and Marie substitutes in elementary school. For all of them, teaching is a serious undertaking, a calling.

What does it mean—to be a teacher?

~ ~ ~

To be a teacher is to share your knowledge and skill so that others can find their way to their own view of truth.

To be a teacher is to care about the questions and have an endless hunger and alertness for the answers.

To be a teacher is to have, in the back of your mind—even on days off—the continuing question, "How can I do it better? relate to them more effectively? share with them my love of the subject without depriving them of the joy of discovering it for themselves?"

To be a teacher is to have an investment in the lives

of those you teach, so that who you are to them is part of the formative equation of their lives.

To be a teacher is to share, in an ongoing way, some of the passion and wisdom of your life.

To be a teacher is to risk your own vulnerability so that others know it's O.K. to make mistakes. Nobody is right all the time.

To be a teacher is to look for the depth in yourself and, from that place, reach out to the depth in another.

~ ~ ~

It is no small task. It was never thought to be. As the bumper sticker says, "If you can read this, thank a teacher."

Chances are, if you are reading this book, you are a teacher. How did you become one?

Maybe it's something you've always wanted to do. Perhaps most children, if their experience of school is at all pleasant, have some fantasies of being "the teacher." I recall lining up rows of chairs in my family's living room, setting the piano stool in front of the first row, assembling a sheaf of lined papers and a red pencil, and playing school. (As an adult, I was surprised to learn that most teachers don't *love* to correct papers. The rustling pages, the curve of the red pencil marks on the paper, were the favorite part of my play.)

Or maybe somewhere along the line — as a Girl Scout leader, a lab assistant, a parent explaining a difficult problem — you realized you have a gift for teaching, or a passion to share the excitement of a particular field of learning or experience.

7

Perhaps you heard that teachers are needed and, thinking about it, something quickened in your heart and mind, and you wondered, "Is this for me — part of my calling as a Christian?"

Then maybe one day the Christian Education director calls as part of the fall recruitment and asks if you've thought about teaching.

Or some Sunday after church, a beleaguered Sunday school superintendent stops you as you're about to leave and says, "When the Millers leave for Idaho next month, we won't have anybody to teach Linda's third-grade class. Could you take over?" Startled, you say, "I'll think about it."

Or maybe you volunteer.

However this call makes itself known to you, you probably have misgivings: "Will I relate well to this group? Do I want to be gone from my own class? Can I take the time to do the necessary preparation?" And, "Am I good enough? If I am to mediate faith to these children (or youth or adults), will I be a presence to draw them to Christ, to the mystery of faith in God?" And you think, and pray, and wonder, and think of the teachers you have had — which ones you remember most fondly and what aspect of their teaching most affected you.

You feel your excitement level rise, and you begin to see yourself in that class, with those people. And you respond, "Yes, I will."

And you begin, knowing this job will take all your resources, wanting the best possible experience for your students and for yourself.

Perhaps teaching turns out to be everything you

had hoped and more. The teacher-training workshops and the study materials give you all the help you need. The students are responsive. You enjoy one another. You feel refreshed and empowered by your contacts with them.

Of course some of the misgivings remain, and sometimes when Saturday night comes and company is there for the weekend and you're tired, you may think, "Why did I ever let myself get into this?"

But then on Sunday, something happens. Some children who always seemed at loggerheads begin to share; an adult who has been sick returns to class and says, "While I was down I remembered what you'd said about God being with us in the night"; a youth you thought was barely tolerating the class, one you'd probably never see again, comes and brings a friend. Then your calling as a teacher is affirmed. And when you relax in the afternoon with the Sunday paper, you sit back, breathe a sigh of relief, and perhaps say a prayer of gratitude for being able to be present to those people in your class — even a prayer for the whole history of faith and family and experience that has brought you this close, again, to the pulsebeat of life with God.

It is an ongoing rise and fall, this business of being a teacher — waves of delight and satisfaction give way to feelings of frustration and fatigue. And finding ways to maintain ourselves, to keep a sense of our own presence, to keep tuned in on God's power to sustain us — this is a constant need in the lives of teachers, and we may find our resolve wearing thin under the strain of constantly being ready for the unexpected, being vulnerable in a setting where we have, at best, a limited control—the strain of sensing, again, the gap between our vision of ourselves as teachers, informing and inspiring our students, and what actually happens.

This book is an attempt to help teachers, in both Sunday schools and weekday schools, keep the springs of refreshment alive and available through prayer and Scripture chosen with teachers particularly in mind, and through the shared experience of other teachers.

"Oh, yes, prayer and Scripture," we say, fully mindful of our need for God's guidance and strength. But it is easy for that awareness to become another demand on our time and interest, and we are already overloaded. So we may put it off, or engage halfheartedly in routine formulas for prayer and Bible reading and hope that will do. And if it doesn't, we feel guilty, indicted for somehow not establishing that connection with God which we know we are supposed to be able to have.

The purpose of this book is to help teachers with prayer and Scripture—not as one more task to complete, but as a way of being, a way of seeing what we are already doing and being, and to suggest and encourage some new ways of prayer—not as a duty to be fulfilled, but as a hunger to be fed.

It is also the hope of those who have shared in the preparation of this book that we can help teachers to relax, to realize that what we offer our students is not some perfect image of an all-competent teacher, but ourselves — as people who also are struggling to know, and to be faithful to, our own gifts.

A friend tells of a voice teacher who cautioned against trying to achieve someone else's voice: "The disciplines of vocal practice are to help you find and strengthen *your* voice."

The seeds of spiritual growth are already in us. And they are to be honored, nurtured, tended, celebrated — as are the lives of the students to whom we offer the holy gift of ourself as teacher. In the words of John Wesley,

> I sit down alone, Only God is here;
> In his presence I open, I read his books;
> And what I thus learn, I teach.

There is a story of a woman who set out on an ocean voyage. She was told by the captain that she could choose her cabin location. Whether out of modest self-esteem or because it was the closest at hand, she settled herself in the hold of the ship and there she stayed, crowded, with poor air and no view, until the journey ended.

At the end of the voyage she came to the upper deck and saw, for the first time, the spacious staterooms, the promenade deck, the tables covered with linen and fine silver. When she was greeted again by the captain he asked her how the voyage had gone. She told him that she'd made it all right, but how crowded it had been, how minimal the food and drink.

He shook his head sadly, indicating with a sweep of his arm the graciousness that surrounded them.

"You could have come up to better accommodations."

We feel sadness for that woman, the sense of "Why didn't I avail myself? It was all there for the taking."

In a way, this is an analogy for us and our yearning for the spiritual life, a life rich in the presence and assurance of God. We know—at least in a part of ourselves—that this richness is available to us if we claim it, put ourselves in line to receive it. But we are busy, and it is too much to contemplate—nurturing one more thing—especially when its results are so nebulous.

Or maybe we have tried to pray, to read Scripture prayerfully. We do it dutifully. After all, we are Christians, and Christians—especially if they are teachers and therefore models, experts—pray and read the Bible. But no aura appears. No voice unmistakably says, "I'm here. I'm real. You've reached me." So, perhaps because we are busy, or because we are threatened by the possibility of failure and therefore the collapse of all we stand for, we pay a nodding toll of a few moments, a few Bible verses read—and move on so we can "get something accomplished."

But we remember. . . . There were times when, in the silence, we felt close to God—and to the whole creation—when somehow the air danced and sang and troubles were muted into tenderness and our lives were made new—in prayer. And perhaps at the time we thought, "I didn't know it was this wonderful, this available—this sense of God being as real as my hand. I'll never lose this connection again."

But we do. We relish the memory of that radiance and for a while are warmed and fed by it. Then unless we are careful, we coast away, back to the absorbing daily minutiae of our lives. And with a faint tug at the heart, we recognize what we have had and let go, and we promise ourselves that one day, when we have more time, we'll settle down and cultivate all that God-reality again. So we stay in the hold, on a minimal diet, and try, as teachers, to relay the love and word of God to people as hungry as we to receive it.

Called to Pray

As teachers, we are called to pray. For how can we relay life in God to others if we let the springs of our own faith dry up?

The disciples knew that prayer was the secret of Jesus' power. They yearned to be like him. "Teach us to pray," they begged. "What is your secret?" they were asking. "We see God in you. Is it possible that we, too . . . ?" And Jesus answered "Yes. You can."

In Sunday school we urge our students to pray. We pray with them. We recommend prayer as an answer to life's troubles and sometime dreariness, as a guide to making choices, as a comfort in times of grief, a restorer of perspective, a power for healing, an opportunity to meet the living God.

We know of Jesus' dependence on prayer, and we read the testimony of saints to the power of prayer in their lives. And we know, from our own experience, that when the biggest crises hit us, we will pray, we will seek God out. And God will be there for us. But in the meantime, we go on our way, making do, meeting our responsibilities, but hungry for a more ardent relationship with God. For we know God is a winsome

God, wanting to be with us more eagerly than we want to be with God.

We *are* busy. Of course. Anyway, all that we do is God's work, isn't it? Especially if we are Sunday school teachers, our commitment to God is clear. Things are going along pretty well. Why rock the boat?

It is a well-founded caution. Maybe we don't want our lives disarranged; and if we pray, who knows what might happen? Even if nothing huge were required of us, we might be asked to change in small ways.

Besides, we are so used to our discomforts and stresses and not sure we want a reprieve — like the people in the story who were invited to throw their troubles into the middle of the room and then choose one to take away with them. Each person, after deliberation, retrieved his or her own. Maybe we are fearful of even a happy transformation — at least for now, until we finish what we are doing and have the energy for any new agenda God might suggest.

There is perhaps another fear: What if we pray, opening our lives to God's power, and nothing significant happens? It would be not only a disappointment, but would threaten our whole worldview! Prayer is basic to the Christian faith. We know faith is a risk, a venture into mystery. If we put it to the test and it failed, the failure would not be ours alone, but that of the faith — the whole thing a ruse — a crisis for us far worse than even the uneasiness that keeps us yearning for God but not trying very hard to reach God. It is like promising ourselves to diet but never starting for fear we may fail.

Little Good in Feeling Guilty

It probably does little good to feel guilty about not doing enough to cultivate the spiritual life. What is enough? I remember hearing a saintly man begin his talk on the spiritual life by saying that he couldn't function well without devoting at least two hours a day to prayer and meditation."Whoa!" I thought. "That's very commendable. But that's too much for me!" And felt, already, slightly second class.

The invitation to pray is not an invitation to a marathon. God is not a Master Coach, standing grim-faced with stopwatch in hand to see who puts in the most time and thereby wins the spirituality contest. One modern writer suggests that Evangelical Protestants have taken on an extra burden of guilt — and the heresy of works-righteousness — by assuming that all serious Christians go apart somewhere and commune easily, productively, freely, joyfully, with God. It's not that easy. The mind wanders, the body frets, there is much "real work" calling to be done.

Ways of Being with God

The invitation to pray is an invitation to be with God. In the rhythms of our lives — from solitude to sociability, from quiet through the various degrees of attending to the sounds of the world, from awareness of our own inner self to a complete absorption in what's going on around us — there are many occasions for being aware of God, of the surprising presence of God in our lives. "Sometimes there's God so quickly," says one of the characters in Tennessee Williams' *Streetcar Named Desire.*

Any of those occasions may evoke prayer from us. In the movie *The Twelve Chairs,* a man who has been searching for a particular chair is running across a field, when suddenly the chair comes wafting down from the sky and lands at his feet."Thank you!" he says in astonishment and delight, and he picks it up and runs on. A quick acknowledgment. A prayer of gratitude.

Prayer As a Way of Looking at Life

As teachers and as Christians, we need to be aware of the holy moments in our lives — not as substitutes for a time apart to pray, but as continually available enrichment of our sense of God.

We remember the words of Brother Lawrence: "The time of business does not with me differ from the time of prayer; and in the noise and clutter of my kitchen, while several persons are at the same time calling for different things, I possess God in as great tranquillity as if I were upon my knees at the blessed sacrament" (*The Practice of the Presence of God* [Revell, 1895], p. 8).

Prayer is a way of looking at life, an attitude of awareness always open to the presence of the Spirit — not as something new (though there will be times when an apt surprise may speak God's name with such freshness it will seem new), but as a steadying ever-available presence — as we turn a handle to bring water from a faucet. Water is there all the time —

available to drink or wash away soil and fatigue. It inhabits the very walls of the house.

Prayer As Paying Attention

Prayer has been described as Paying Attention. If we are people who pay attention, we are aware of God in the numinousness of everyday events: the arrival of a letter or a book; a phone call when we need it most; an appearance at the door of a loved friend when grief is eating at our heart — "I was going by and felt I wanted to stop and see how you're doing." Tears and healing, Christ mediated to us through those who love us — all are invitations to be with God, a kind of prayer. Frederick Buechner, in *The Alphabet of Grace,* writes of this kind of event: "We tend to go on as though nothing has happened. To go on as though something *has* happened . . . is to enter that dimension of life that religion is a word for" (The Seabury Press, 1970, p. 76). The numinous in the everyday — prayer as Paying Attention.

The Class As Blessed Community

Our Sunday school classes are not only places for teaching about God, they are holy communities where healing and love and support act out God's love for us.

A young father brings his four-year-old daughter to Sunday school. He says, "We just took Charlotte's mother to the airport for a business trip. After the plane took off, Charlotte said, 'Now I'm going to my

class. I want someone to give me a hug and a kiss.' "
He adds, "It's the first time she hasn't cried when her
mother left."

An adult Sunday school class postpones its
scheduled lesson to ask instead that the teacher help
them discern how they can minister to one of their
members who has recently been diagnosed as having
cancer.

A junior high boy speaks up in a discussion of the
elderly: "We can learn a lot from old people." I, the
teacher, think how proud his parents and grand-
parents would be, and I feel my own affection and
regard for older adults enlarged.

On the way into Sunday school, some children have
spotted a wounded bird. They tell me about it and we
go out to see. The bird cannot fly. We find a box, line
it with soft grass and, tenderly, move the bird into the
box and take it to the veterinarian around the corner.
He is kind, sympathetic, but he cannot save the bird,
and it dies as we watch. We take it back and bury it in
the churchyard. We stand quietly. Today, this is the
lesson — occasions lived in acknowledgment of the
presence of God.

The Beauty of the Physical World

The astonishing beauty of our world also leads us
to a consciousness of God's presence. We savor this
and sometimes share it with our students — snow on
telephone wires and tree limbs, a bird building a nest
under our eaves, the combination of colors in a woven

blanket, the shape of a vase. The sensitizing quality of objects — occasions for a prayer of gratitude.

Sometimes we are tempted to think of objects as not being important. It is one of the tragedies of the homeless that they have no objects to mean continuity, personal history, home.

"Steep yourself in the sea of matter. . . for it is the source of your life," writes the Jesuit priest Pierre Teilhard de Chardin. He continues, "You hoped that the more thoroughly you rejected the tangible, the closer you would be to the spirit. . . . Well, you were like to have perished of hunger" (*Hymn of the Universe* [Harper & Row, 1965], pp. 63-64). All these wonders feed the teacher's storehouse of energy and spiritual resource.

Times of Worship

Corporate worship, when the presence of the community of believers supports our impulse to pray, will help to fill our reservoir of faith.

Blessings Before Meals. One physiologist suggests that the moment of blessing serves a healthful physical function by quieting our systems, preparing them to receive food.

Prayers Upon Waking, Prayers Before Going to Sleep. These prayers are often perfunctory, but still usefully undergird our nights and days — a kind of checking in with God, an acknowledgment that all we do is done in God's presence.

All these suggest that our lives are as porous to God as we are to the air we breathe. When as teachers we think of ways prayer and other aspects of spiritual discipline can strengthen and enrich us for the task, as well as benefit our own lives, we do well to remember that prayer is not something to be done for fifteen minutes a day, or five, or one hundred twenty, if we are like the sainted scholar to whom I referred. Prayer is an attitude of being attentive to God, entertaining the possibility that at any moment God, who is always present in our lives, may make a particular gesture of Presence, and that we do well to be on the lookout.

Spiritual Discipline—A Time Apart

But there is another aspect of God-attentiveness that lays claim to our lives. What about a time apart for prayer, meditation, reading?

At some seasons in our lives, the best we can manage for private prayer may be a few moments at bedtime or upon rising. Then we rely on corporate worship and maybe, through the day, an occasional quick prayer of gratitude and supplication—our acknowledgment that God's power and presence infuse the world. One writer has likened this to a relationship with a dear friend one sees only sporadically, but when one does, the relationship is immediately there in all its richness, history, and support.

But most of us can find the time if we want to. Perhaps when the children are small or under the duress of a particular crisis, the time is not available. But usually it is our own will, not the clock, that interferes with time spent in prayer, meditation, and reading of the Scriptures. And we have a nagging feeling that we could be better people, better teachers and doers of the Word, if we had a richer life of communion with God. Maybe later, when things aren't so busy. . . .

Perhaps we recognize, with a start, the words of Emilie Griffin: "There is a moment between intending to pray and actually praying that is as dark and silent as any moment in our lives. It is the split second between thinking about prayer and really praying. For some of us, this split second may last for decades" (*Clinging: The Experience of Prayer* [Harper & Row, 1984], p. 1).

To leave ourselves open to extended periods of prayer is to leave ourselves open. In *Reaching Out,* Henri Nouwen writes: "The movement from illusion to prayer is hard to make since it leads us from false certainties to true uncertainties, from an easy support system to a risky surrender, and from the many 'safe' gods to the God whose love has no limits" (Doubleday, 1975, p. 165). There is a lot at stake.

But whether prompted by witnesses from without or hunger from within, most Christians find themselves drawn to times of quiet solitude — to refresh their spirits, to plumb, nourish, and celebrate their relationship with God.

The Way to Begin Is to Begin

We decide to try, or try again, to deliberately seek out God, to give ourselves to the mystery of God's presence, the possibility of God's availability. How can we keep those times fresh — periods of insight and power? And if they're not? What do we do then?

One could fill a large room with books on this subject — how to design and maintain times of prayer and meditation. But there is a way in which no guidebook is ever the right book, or the right book for long, and, as teachers, we must use our best teacherly wisdom to find a "lesson plan" that will work for us.

The God Who Waits for Us

The purpose of spiritual discipline is to help us find our way to the God who waits for us.

"Always there is a dream dreaming us," a Bushman told Laurens van der Post *(The Heart of the Hunter* [Wm. Morrow & Co., 1961], pp. 151-52). In *Shaped by the Word,* Robert Mulholland refers to each of us as "a 'word' spoken forth by God" (The Upper Room, 1985, p. 36).

How to envision the dream? How can we claim that reality of ourselves as "words" spoken forth by God?

The first requisite, of course, is to set aside some time. Do the mechanics matter — the setting, the time? Sometimes they do, sometimes they don't. But we probably will increase our chances of success if we attend to them.

A quiet place, then. And if we can return to the same place each day, the association will help lead us into the mood for prayer. Some people find that a particular picture or piece of sculpture helps to establish the right mood. Some find a symbolic exercise a help — washing one's hands before entering the "quiet space," as a symbol of freeing oneself from the cares of the day, for example.

What time? A time when we can be free to relax, be attentive to what comes to us from the silence. Time enough not to feel rushed. Many people find early morning a good time. (In monastic orders morning prayers often begin at 4 A.M.!) Some find a quiet time in late afternoon a good transition from the rush of the day to the different character of evening. Some prefer the close of day, just before going to bed.

It is important to be comfortable (though not so at ease that we fall asleep!) and to have adequate fresh air. A few moments of measured deep breathing or some Yoga exercises may be a good beginning. We often carry our tensions in the diaphragm, the lower jaw, the back of the neck. It is helpful to consciously relax those areas of the body.

Patterns for a Time of Prayer

Then, What to Do? Many people are afraid of unprogrammed time. We can sympathize with the philosopher who took a job as a house painter so he would have something to do while he was thinking. We are told that the desert Fathers became basket weavers — not only to provide themselves a means of income, but to give them something to occupy the time.

So it probably is a good idea to have some pattern — a sequence of events in mind when we approach a period of prayer. Reuben Job and Norman Shawchuck, in *A Guide to Prayer for Ministers and Other Servants* (The Upper Room, 1983), suggest the following outline (pp. 5-11):

Invocation

Psalm

Daily Scripture Readings

Readings for Reflection (other than Scripture)

Prayers

Reflection [including writing in a personal journal what you have experienced—any thoughts, hopes, plans—and your periods of dryness as well as times of exhilaration]

Hymn

For each of these components, the authors have included initial commentary and excellent day-by-day, week-by-week selections, following the seasons of the church year.

Other books of this kind are available—as well as published lists from the interdenominational lectionary (selected Scripture readings to cover the Bible in a three-year cycle).

In prayer workbooks for use by individuals or covenant groups, specific exercises are suggested as well as modes of discussion and sharing. (Teachers, who are familiar with workbooks containing fill-in-the-blanks pages, may find this approach especially pleasing—only this time we are the students, not the teachers!)

In any suggested scheme for private worship, we may want to change the order from time to time. Sometimes a single sentence or phrase, a thought, a portion of Scripture, or a prayer, will move us through the curtain of illusion into the presence of the God who waits for us.

Often a reading for reflection prepares the way for appreciation of a Scripture passage. In *Preaching and Preachers,* D. Martyn Lloyd-Jones writes:

> I have come to learn certain things about private prayer. You cannot pray to order. You can get on your knees to order; but how to pray? I have found nothing more important than to learn how to get oneself into that frame and condition in which one can pray. You have to learn how to start yourself off, and it is just here that this knowledge of yourself is so important. What I have generally found is that to read something which can be characterised in general as devotional is of great value. . . . Notice that I do not say that you should start yourself in prayer by always reading the Scriptures; because you can have precisely the same difficulty there. Start by reading something that will warm your spirit. Get rid of a coldness that may have developed in your spirit. You have to learn how to kindle a flame in your spirit. . . . It is comparable, if you like, to starting a car when it is cold. You have to learn how to use a spiritual choke. I have found it most rewarding to do that, and not to struggle vainly. When one finds oneself in this condition, and that it is difficult to pray, do not struggle in prayer for the time being, but read something that will warm and stimulate you, and you will find that it will put you into a condition in which you will be able to pray more freely. (Zondervan, 1971, p. 170)

How to read Scriptures? We, as Sunday school teachers, try to pass the treasure of the Scriptures on to our pupils — both as a record of the church's history and as a way to see God in the world now. As

Christian teachers, in whatever setting, we want our lives and those of our students to be filled with the light and love of God as seen in the Scriptures. The richness of the Scriptures would take a lifetime to appreciate, but sometimes we may be hard pressed to find in a particular passage the luminous window to God we believe is there.

What scheme to follow? Most of us probably foundered long ago on any oft-conceived but seldom-completed scheme to "read the Bible all the way through." We might choose one of the lectionary listings or the passages suggested in some study or devotional guide we are using. An excellent way to incorporate our teaching material into our inner life, if we are Sunday school teachers, is to use the Bible material in the lesson for Sunday. This familiarizes us with the passages for the day, and may, if we read and ponder and dwell upon the passages, help us to so ingest them into our own nature that we will relay them to our students in a more profound way than a more cursory examination would evoke.

The phrase "praying the Scriptures" describes a meditative, free-association way to incorporate Bible passages and stories into our lives and is useful for any student of the Bible. After choosing a Scripture passage, one starts with a prayer of "centering," in which one relaxes the body and spirit, asks for an awareness of God's presence, and chooses a word or phrase as a simple reminder of God. Without strain, one returns to that word as the mind wanders off, until after a few moments one feels centered, untrammeled, attentive. Then one reads the Scripture slowly, reflectively, lingering on any images that seem particularly meaningful or arresting. For example, when Psalm 131, with its image of the child resting in its mother's arms, is read in this way, one feels some of the tension of life drop away.

Imagine yourself into the Scripture, into the role of different figures in the story. How would they feel?

Read about the birth of Moses (Exod. 2:1-8) and imagine you are the sister, watching from the reeds while the king's daughter comes to the river and sees your brother, Moses, in the basket! Or imagine, in Jesus' story of the lost son (Luke 15:11-32), that you are the son returning home, dejected and fearful. Then imagine you are the elder brother, wondering why your father is making such a fuss when you have been faithful and dutiful all this time. Imagine you are the aged father, and you see on the horizon the figure of the son you'd given up for lost!

What if you had been one of the first of the five thousand (John 6:1-13) to receive food; one of the last?

What do these stories tell us about God's relationship to us, and ours to one another? Sometimes an action suggests itself, sometimes an insight.

After you have absorbed whatever the Scripture has to offer, you might conclude with a prayer of gratitude for the leadings of the day, and for the company of believers who, in a symbolic sense, have been present to this Scripture, nourished by these words. Then perhaps you will want to move on to other readings for reflection, other forms of prayer.

Lectio Divina

The sixth-century Benedictines developed a fourfold way of experiencing and praying the Scriptures which seems as germane to our times as it must have seemed when first they used it. The process is known as *lectio divina*, having to do with the inspired Word of God.

It is based on the belief that the Scriptures are the basic food for the Christian, that we come to know God through God's Word, that to be reconciled to God—to have "the mind of Christ"—we must steep ourselves in the memory, the history, the stories, the moods, and the traditions of God's action in the world. Scripture is our "family story"; it tells us where we come from and who we are.

The Four Phases of "Lectio Divina"

1. *Lectio*: getting acquainted with the text, both informationally (its content) and formationally (its effect on us when we give ourselves to it).
2. *Meditatio* (not meditation): rumination; memorization, or making the contents one's own. This is the process of ingesting the Scripture, entering the memory of God's action—a union between heart and mind, in which we allow the Scripture to speak to us at the deepest level, to form our thinking and speaking. We "learn it by heart," to use an old pedagogic term!
3. *Oratio*: prayer that responds to the Word of God. When we become acquainted with the Word of

---

God, we become acquainted with God—as friends are known to one another through their words. So we make some response to the God we are glimpsing—of adoration, praise, intercession, or of commitment as to what we resolve to do or to be.

4. *Contemplatio*: being at ease in the Presence without much need for words or thought. This is a kind of unitive state, in which we are taken out of ourselves and experience a sense of wonder, of awe, of communion with God. A human analogy might be the communion of marriage partners who have been together for so long they often understand and relish each other's presence without need for words.

Prayer in Spiritual Discipline

There is, of course, a lot of overlap between prayer and reading of Scripture in the ways described above. There is overlap between prayer and much else that we do. The same kind of inner attending to the springs of creativity that occurs when authors give themselves to the writing of a story, or a sculptor shapes clay or stone, or a composer searches for the perfect note, has much in common with the prayer of waiting, of listening for God. The words of Brother Lawrence quoted earlier describe a kind of dual level of living in which one attends to business while at the same time retaining an ongoing communion with God.

But when we have gone to our private space, and after we have read the Scriptures, what form do our prayers take?

Prayer of Gratitude

Perhaps it is well to start with a prayer of gratitude — for being alive; for the support of faith and friends and family; for having work to do; for the astonishing possibility of having a relationship with God, who is both Lord of the universe and "nearer than breathing, closer than hands and feet" — gratitude for the gifts one is aware of at the time. For teachers, it is a gift (though it may not always seem so!) to have access to the minds and hearts of students. Let's be grateful, then, for our students and for the opportunity to be present to them.

Prayer of Intercession

We have things on our minds — people we love who are in difficulty, a world where violence and injustice are daily scourges. We remember these in prayer. We pray for ourselves and our own needs, and certainly for our students.

Years ago when I was student teaching, I attended meetings of the teachers and the supervising professor. A chief feature of these meetings was a process called "staffing," in which we discussed a particular child — usually one who seemed to be having difficulty.

In the confidentiality of the gathered group, the child's life circumstances were described, behavior and developmental problems were presented, times of stress were noted. We talked about how the child responded to various periods in the school day—free play, story time, the play yard, lunch, rest period, the time when a parent came to pick the child up. Then we proposed what we might do to enhance the child's growth, self-esteem, and joy in the school day.

What happened, of course, was that we all left the meeting with an abundance of love and understanding for this child—who may have been driving us crazy a few hours before—and the will to relate to the child in new and creative ways. "To know all is to forgive all."

So as we pray for the pupils in our class, we would do well to spend particular time on those who may be causing us difficulty—visualizing the student, holding him or her before God, whose love is all-healing, all-compassionate.

In a women's sharing group, a mother who is also a teacher was at her wits' end to deal with the problems her daughter was having in school. Each member of the sharing group was given a piece of clay and told to let her inner spirit direct the shape her hands gave to the clay. After the exercise, the mother, in tears, put on the table a figure of a woman praying over a sleeping child.

"I've tried everything," she said. "Isn't it strange that the last thing you think of is prayer?"

In the wisdom of God's love, prayers of intercession change us. And we are promised that, in the mysterious flow of energy that moves through our world, our prayers can effect change in those for whom we pray. Surely there is room, in the creative flux and flow of the universe, for the energies we release in prayer to enter that stream and make a difference.

Flora Slosson Wuellner, in *Prayer and Our Bodies,* tells that during a meeting, she experienced acute pain in her lower back:

> I sat next to a minister who, through neurological illness, had lost the use of his legs and was sitting in an electric wheelchair. He had a most observable loving radiance about him. In the midst of the meeting, my pain suddenly and dramatically left me.
>
> "Did you pray for me?" I asked him afterwards.
>
> "Yes," he answered quietly. "I observed that you were in discomfort, and I channeled God's healing light to you."
>
> "Has this happened before?" I asked.
>
> He hesitated, and then said, "Yes, I have noticed that sometimes God can use me to help others." (The Upper Room, 1987, p. 91)

She doesn't suggest–and the man in the wheelchair is ample evidence that it is not so–that prayer will heal all our afflictions. We don't know why it sometimes works and sometimes doesn't. We have everything to gain and nothing to lose by trying. Theologian Karl Barth, in discussing the issue of whether we are attempting the impossible in intercessory prayer, suggests that prayer is simply asking. No guarantees. But we have permission–indeed, it is a command–to ask. As Barth pointed out, the prayer Jesus taught us contains six petitions, plus an address and a doxology.

Jesus' prayer in the garden as he foresaw his own crucifixion is the supreme example of a prayer of asking: "If you will, take this cup away from me. Not my will, however, but your will be done" (Luke 22:42 GNB). Then, we are told, "An angel from heaven appeared to him and strengthened him" (Luke 22:43). Did he cease to struggle then? Was everything peaceful? No. "In great anguish he prayed even more fervently; his sweat was like drops of blood, falling to the ground" (Luke 22:44).

There are times when no amount of prayer can remove suffering. It is helpful to remember we are not alone, that Christ, too, suffered uncertainty and his own sense of the absence of God. But in obedience — which may mean a difficult action or the acceptance of an unacceptable reality — lies the way to a resurrection of new life, and of hope.

Prayers for the Church and the World

We pray for the church, for discernment in understanding our responsibility for the larger world — the environment, the hungry and powerless — and for obedience in carrying out that responsibility.

Prayer As Companionship

A child, writing of her experience of God as she suffered from a debilitating illness from which was no recovery, pondered the meaning of her life: "God wants me for company."

There is a kind of prayer that has no aim but itself: prayer in which one has a sense of ultimate Arrival, of blessed assurance that one is encompassed in Life, relishing the presence of the Other; that whatever eternal life means, this moment has a quality that seems to reach through time and space and strike a resonant chord.

This is perhaps the ultimate form of prayer, the most exhilarating, the most enabling. It has been likened to being in the presence of one so dearly loved, so known, that few if any words are necessary. A woman long schooled in prayer was asked to describe what happened during her long periods of contemplation. Her answer: "I look at God and God looks at me."

This kind of prayer appears as a gift, a surprise, an energizing blessing. The striving ceases, the thinking, the struggle to formulate words and concepts ends.

If it is so rewarding, why is such prayer so hard to attain? Perhaps it comes upon us only after a history of absorbing Scripture, the holy community, the give and take of life.

Perhaps we expect the wrong things in prayer, and so we keep ourselves distant from God — like straining to see a bus approaching when it is coming from the opposite direction.

The Prayer of the Heart

Henri Nouwen, in *The Way of the Heart* (Seabury Press, 1981), speaks of some of the deterrents to this kind of prayer. They are deterrents perhaps particularly for teachers, for whom discourse and the life of the mind are so important:

> For many of us prayer means nothing more than speaking with God. And since it usually seems to be a quite one-sided affair, prayer simply means talking to God. This idea is enough to create great frustrations. If I present a problem, I expect a solution; if I formulate a question, I expect an answer; if I ask for guidance, I expect a response. And when it seems, increasingly, that I am talking into the dark, it is not so strange that I soon begin to suspect that my dialogue with God is in fact a monologue. Then I begin to ask myself: To whom am I really speaking, God or myself? (p. 72)

A second deterrent, after speaking what appears to be a monologue, is restricting prayer to thoughts about God:

> The basic conviction is that what is needed is to think thoughts about God and his mysteries. Prayer therefore requires hard mental work and is quite fatiguing. . . . Since we already have so many other practical and pressing things on our minds, thinking about God becomes one more demanding burden. This is especially true because thinking about God is not a spontaneous event, while thinking about pressing concerns comes quite naturally. (p. 73)

Nouwen goes on to commend the Prayer of the Heart as taught and practiced by the Desert Fathers.

> From the heart arise unknowable impulses as well as conscious feelings, moods, and wishes. The heart, too,

has its reasons and is the center of perception and understanding. Finally, the heart is the seat of the will:
it makes plans and comes to good decisions. Thus the
heart is the central and unifying organ of our personal
life. . . . It is this heart that is the place of prayer. The
prayer of the heart is a prayer that directs itself to God
from the center of the person and thus affects the
whole of our humanness. . . . The most profound insight of the Desert Fathers is that entering into the
heart is entering into the kingdom of God. (p. 77-78)

The Prayer of the Heart, the prayer of rest, a bring-
ing of all that we are — thought, emotion, daily agenda, long-term anxiety, hope, fear, will — into the
all-seeing, all-embracing Presence of God, so that we
are wholly present and an undivided resting of the
total self is possible. It is this undivided nature of the
encounter that makes it a "prayer of rest."

Keeping It Going

How to keep it going? Perhaps a parallel with learning is appropriate. Learning takes time, discipline,
persistence. And so does prayer, the life of the spirit.

The chief incentive to continue will be our success — our sense of being in closer touch with God and
with ourselves; a sense of peace under stress, of
clearer direction for our lives; maybe some unexpected breakthroughs with students. Even so, we will
have dry periods, and for a while may abandon our
spiritual disciplines in the press of daily living. But
the sense of being at-home-in-God, our memory of
luminous times, will call to us.

"Prayer is a matter of keeping at it," writes Emilie Griffin. "The rewards will come no other way" (*Clinging*, p. 9). What to do when we begin well enough, have some gratifying experiences, but then, regretfully, begin to drift away again? What are some ways to nourish spiritual discipline, in addition to our own good resolution?

Maybe we are trying too hard. Perhaps it is difficult to relax and wait for God. We fill the silence with our own thoughts, fearful that if we don't, the silence will be empty—we will discover no one else there. In *Merton's Palace of Nowhere,* James Finley recalls a conversation with Thomas Merton:

> Merton once told me to quit trying so hard in prayer. He said, "How does an apple ripen? It just sits in the sun." A small green apple cannot ripen in one night by tightening all its muscles, squinting its eyes and tightening its jaw in order to find itself the next morning miraculously large, red, ripe and juicy beside its small green counterparts. Like the birth of a baby or the opening of a rose, the birth of the true self takes place in God's time. We must wait for God, we must be awake; we must trust in his hidden action within us.([Ave Maria Press, 1978], pp. 115-16)

We can experiment with different kinds of prayer. We have already described in some detail the modes of *lectio divina.* In *The Breath of Life,* Ron Del Bene describes the Breath Prayer—a way for each person to use his or her own most present need of God as a prayer to fill the interstices of the day. Basil Pennington's *Centering Prayer* describes fully the process briefly alluded to earlier. Some people have chosen a common daily event to remind them of God—the ringing of the bell that marks the beginning and end of a class, the turning on of a light.

Retreats. An increasing number of retreat centers have sprung up around the country, many with persons available for spiritual counseling. A retreat at least once a year is a good way to refresh one's commitment to spiritual discipline. Churches often plan a "day apart," which allows time for personal reflection and growth.

Faith Friends. Some congregations have an ongoing program, a pairing, for a stated interval (perhaps six months), of people who meet weekly to share faith journeys and encourage each other.

A Covenant Group. Similar to faith friends, except the group is larger and may have an agreed-upon discipline of lectionary readings, prayer, or other forms of spiritual discipline. They meet at stated intervals for sharing and accountability.

Literature. Many books on spiritual growth are available. Find some that speak to your needs.

Simplification of Life. It is hard to find time and energy to "wait for God" when one is rushing about in a frenzy. Simplifying our life not only gives us time for prayer, but enables us to be alert to occasions where others may need us. One reason suggested for the Samaritan's ability to stop and help the wounded and robbed traveler: He had time — he wasn't rushing to a meeting!

Journal Keeping. When we write down responses to what we have read, our own experience with prayer and Scripture, this not only gives us a record of our spiritual life, but the act of recording helps assimilate and fix in the mind what has happened — or not happened.

Cultivation of Obedience. We can obey what Quaker theologian Douglas Steere calls "the nudges" of God, the small things — a phone call made, a book read, a moment of spontaneous prayer and acknowledgment. Such obedience reinforces growth, sustains our belief in the power of the Spirit to lead us.

If we experience a period of extended dryness, we can do some extra act of "good works" — help out with a program for the homeless, gather some no-longer needed clothes and give them away, make an extra visit to the elderly. By acting in ways that seem especially compatible with God's love for the world, we draw closer to that love ourselves and are refreshed.

We are promised that if we persist, we will win through, that something is going on. Just as children are unaware of growing, some growth is taking place in us. As seeds lie in the dark earth, God is using our darkness, our period of dryness, to prepare us for new growth. "The goal, in darkness," says Emilie Griffin, "is not to whimper about it, but to live it, while it lasts, as deeply as any other gift God gives us in experience. One day, without knowing how or why, something has lifted. The darkness has simply gone away" (*Clinging,* p. 27).

~ ~ ~

Remember, always, that prayer is a mystery, the possibility of encounter with the Power of life. And we are not acting alone. In this exchange in which we sometimes feel unheard, our faith, the testimony of Scripture, and the history of the church assure us that God is dwelling within us. It is out of that confidence that, unworthy as we sometimes feel, we are called to be teachers — telling, showing, trying, failing — but knowing that the Giver of life has called us to bring in a many-faceted way — through words and film and dance, silence and laboratory experiment, scissors and construction paper and paste, computer and typewriter and camera — some reflection of the glory of the Lord, to be handed from teacher to student and back again, with infinite listening and teaching and patience and love.

DIRECTION FROM SCRIPTURE

Lead Me in Thy Truth, and Teach Me

Show me thy ways, O LORD; teach me thy paths:
Lead me in thy truth, and teach me:
for thou art the God of my salvation;
on thee do I wait all the day.
(Psalm 25:4-5 KJV)

These words of the psalmist reveal two qualities indispensable to a worthy teacher. The first is the sense of personal inadequacy that must fill the heart of any teacher who takes the job seriously. "Who is equal to these things?" — this is the cry of anyone who honestly attempts to introduce other minds to the inexhaustible wealth of knowledge, or seeks to lead them into the deep resources of spiritual power. Only a confirmed egotist can feel adequate. But humble souls, conscious of their inadequacies, can face the task in the knowledge that when they have done their best, poor though it may be, God has a way of using it beyond its intrinsic worth to communicate the truth and fulfill the purposes of God.

Many times in the course of a long ministry, when I preached what I knew to be a poor sermon, some grateful soul would say, "You spoke to my need today. You gave me the help I needed." And I knew it was not my words, but that God was using my words, poor as they were, to speak his message. This is the assurance of all teachers who offer their best to God.

The other quality of a worthy teacher revealed in this prayer is a teachable spirit: "Lead me in thy truth, and teach me." This is what Christ means when he said to his disciples, "Learn of me." A teachable spirit is not merely open to the facts of our biblical heritage, or the possibility of new interpretations of Scripture, but seeks to learn and appropriate that Spirit which came in its fullness in Christ.

Have you ever asked yourself, "What is the essence of Christianity?" It is not just a philosophy of life, though the faith of Jesus is ultimately the only thing that can make sense of the universe. It is not just a moral code, though it provides the most sublime and noble ethic in the world. The essence of Christianity is neither of these. It is a personal attachment — to know and to respond in love to the most fascinating personality who ever walked this earth.

The biographer of that tragic genius Thomas Wolfe tells us that at age twenty-five, Wolfe fell madly in love with Aline Bernstein, almost ten years his senior. On one occasion he wrote her, "I shall love you all the days of my life, and when I die if they cut me open

43

they will find one name written on my brain and in my heart. It will be yours."

In a far more profound sense, the essence of Christianity is some such relationship with Jesus Christ. If Christ is to find a place in our hearts, it will not be because we daily bombard the gates of heaven, but because we wait quietly before him each day, seeking to lay our lives open to his Spirit and fan to flame the frail spark of love for him in our hearts. It is only as we learn his Spirit that we can teach it. It is only as we incarnate his Spirit that the words we speak will touch another human heart with transforming power.

—R. Kern Eutsler

But When You Pray . . .

When his disciples asked about prayer, Jesus proved to be an excellent teacher. Instead of a direct answer, he offered two models.

First he pointed to people the disciples could see — the outwardly religious people who covered their heads with ashes and dressed in sackcloth, the common symbols of repentance and contrition. They loudly declaimed prayers while they attended synagogue services or stood on streetcorners. Their piety was more for outward show than an honest expression of devotion to God.

Jesus offered an alternative: "When you pray, go into your room and shut the door and pray to your Father who is in secret; and your Father who sees in secret will reward you. And in praying do not heap up empty phrases as the Gentiles do; for they think that they will be heard for their many words" (Matt. 6:6-7 RSV).

He followed that with a pattern to be used in his followers' own prayer time with God. We call it The Lord's Prayer (Matt. 6:9b-13 KJV).

Our Father which art in heaven,	Acknowledge God as the one to whom you pray.
Hallowed be thy name.	Honor and praise God.
Thy kingdom come. Thy will be done in earth, as it is in heaven.	Commit yourself to the priorities and causes of God.
Give us this day our daily bread.	Ask God for what you need honestly and plainly.
And forgive us our debts,	Admit your need for repentance, confession, and forgiveness.
As we forgive our debtors.	Recognize that we must give to others what we wish to receive.
And lead us not into temptation, but deliver us from evil:	Ask for protection from temptation and evil, admitting that its power is great and real.
For thine is the kingdom, and the power, and the glory, for ever. Amen.	Offer your adoration and praise again to God, Creator and Sustainer of all.

In this prayer we acknowldge a power and source of creativity and goodness greater than ourselves. We commit ourselves to the ways and causes of God and place these priorities squarely in the midst of our other requests and petitions.

In reflecting about our needs in the presence of God, we gain amazing insight and clarity. We also recognize those things we can do little to change.

We remember that Jesus, in the Garden of Gethsemane, ended his prayer by handing his life over to God with words of humble obedience: "Nevertheless, not as I will, but as thou wilt" (Matt. 26:39 RSV). He had learned that in God's care and keeping, his life had always found its greatest meaning and possibility, and he was willing to trust God in this crucial matter as well.

We who teach would do well to keep Jesus' examples of prayer and obedience before us, to recognize the priorities among our many tasks, never neglecting the Source of our talents, our abilities, and our calling.

—Calvin D. McConnell

Teach Me Wisdom in My Secret Heart

Behold, thou desirest truth in the inward being;
therefore teach me wisdom in my secret heart.
(Psalm 51:6 RSV)

God, I don't feel very wise. Life isn't simple any more. I get confused about who or what to believe. I don't always trust myself to say what I think and feel.

Sometimes I feel like Lazarus—who I really am is shut up in darkness. There's a heaviness that keeps me from your light.

I barely hear you say my name. Keep calling! Give me courage to bring into your light that part of me I want to keep hidden. Remind me that you love me and that your grace helps others love me. I want to become the person you created me to be.

(Take time now to name the things about you which you have thought God would not accept. Listen for God's response.)

Yet, since you love sincerity of heart,
teach me the secrets of wisdom.
(Psalm 51:6 JB)

God, sometimes I feel like Sarah, laughing at your promises. It doesn't seem possible that all you have promised could come to be. I laugh because of my insecurity, I giggle to mask my lack of faith. I smile rather than cry. How will I ever be wise? Turn my nervous laughter into joy, my faithlessness into trust, my teary smile into confident radiance. Remind me that when I trust your promises, I know a secret of wisdom.

(Talk with God now about a promise you have difficulty believing. Listen for God's response.)

Sincerity and truth are what you require;
fill my mind with your wisdom.
(Psalm 51:6 GNB)

I want to know it all. I think I've done what you want me to do. So I pat myself on the back and self-righteously ask you what else there could be for me to know or to do. Carry me across the abyss of my own misunderstanding. Temper my cockiness with humility. Create in me a desire for your truth. Open my mind to your truth. Every day, reveal to me some new way to practice obedience to your truth. Invite me to dance with others in the joy of your revelation. Remind me that you have given me the gift of wisdom: I can claim it when I am truly with you.

(In your mind, picture your classroom and students. Talk with God about the joy you find in teaching, some concerns you have about a student, and what you want to know more about. Listen for God's response.)

—*Cecile A. Beam*

Teach Me Good Judgment and Knowledge

Teach me good judgment and knowledge,
for I believe in thy commandments.
(Psalm 119:66 RSV)

The psalmist is probably using the term *good judgment* very much as we would use *common sense.* All of us who teach in the church certainly need that!

One of the compliments I treasure from my high school days is the caption by my picture in the school annual. It read, "A little common sense is worth a bushel of learning." I am not sure I would want to set common sense and learning against each other. They may very well go together. However, the teacher who exercises good judgment will need a good portion of common sense to understand the learners and to help them apply the gospel to everyday life.

And what about knowledge? The writer of this psalm obviously felt that knowledge is important if one is to believe the Commandments. Knowledge, in the Hebrew sense, was more than facts of the mind; it also included the dimensions of the heart. *Knowing God* meant more than having the objective view that God *is*. It meant to know God in a more intimate, heart-felt sense.

An outstanding United Methodist pastor, the late Harold Bosley, once said, "We are called to be literate citizens of our whole Christian tradition." The wise teacher will seek to become more literate in the Scripture, in church history, and in church traditions and beliefs.

Fortunately, those of us who are called to teach in the church are not expected to have perfect judgment and complete knowledge. We *are* called, however, to continue to grow in our good judgment and to expand our knowledge of the things of God.

Lord, help me to exercise good judgment in my teaching and in my relationships with those I have been called to teach. Help me also, wise and gracious God, to seek to grow in knowledge and in love of you and the neighbor. In the name of the Good and Wise Savior, Jesus Christ our Lord. Amen.

—*Roy H. Ryan*

Teach Me the Way

In thee I put my trust.
Teach me the way I should go,
for to thee I lift up my soul.
(Psalm 143:8 RSV)

The church's teaching ministry communicates the fundamental Christian beliefs, passes on the Christian tradition, and shares the good news of God's love.

In Psalm 143, the psalmist describes how God's love enables him to love his neighbor. He is persuaded that he will never be deprived of God's power, no matter how sinful he may be. Knowing his sinful nature, he relies totally upon God's steadfast love, which supplies the strength to face what he must deal with in life.

The psalmist expresses his willingness to listen to God: "Teach me the way I should go." "Teach me the way" can mean "Be my guide." But Christian teachers must go one step further. The teaching ministry must open the door to the truth that Christ is the way God comes to us and the way we come to God.

The psalmist confesses that we are soiled, sin-stained, guilt-ridden. The good news is that we have the Christ. Christ is the way God comes to us to lift our broken lives with strong arms, carrying us into God's new life.

And the teaching ministry is our own life. As a teacher I must be aware that teaching is closely related to what I say and what I do. What I say and what I do is a mirrored reflection of who I am. Teachers should be confronted by God's way; this confrontation with God keeps our faith alive, and when we are alive in faith, we experience God's gift of a new and better life. Without experiencing this newness, we will lose the dynamics of the meaning of life. The psalmist simply describes this confrontation: "To thee I lift up my soul."

—*Dal Joon Won*

The Holy Spirit ... Will Teach You All Things

The Holy Spirit, whom the Father will send in my name ... will teach you all things, and bring to your remembrance all that I have said to you. Peace I leave with you; my peace I give to you.
(John 14:26-27a RSV)

No teacher can "go it alone." Jesus, the world's greatest teacher, relied on quiet times alone with God. Therefore, on his last night with his disciples, he left them a teaching to sustain them during the difficult times ahead. Listen to Jesus' words:

"The Holy Spirit, whom the Father will send in my name ...." God sent me into the world, and the powers of violence, darkness, sin, and death cannot overcome God's purpose. My Spirit will continue to be with you in the midst of the worst that life can bring.

"The Holy Spirit ... will teach you all things." In three short years, I could not teach you everything. You and all the teachers who come after you will face new challenges, new opportunities, new dangers. But my Spirit will be with you. Be still, and open your mind and your heart to the Spirit's guidance for teaching, for guiding today's learners.

"The Holy Spirit ... will ... bring to your remembrance all that I have said to you." Don't be anxious about what you will teach and how you will teach. Prepare yourself with diligence and love, as you would if I were observing your class, for I am there. Know my teachings; then trust my Spirit to so guide you

that my wisdom and my love may flow through you to your students.

"Peace I leave with you; my peace I give to you." Whatever the subject, whomever you teach, you need the sustaining power of my peace. It sets you free from frantic haste, from irritation, from feeling over-burdened, from feeling inadequate. It tells you that you are not alone. When you are sustained by my peace, your students know they can trust the power that upholds the earth and binds all things together in love.

When Jesus prayed, "I do not pray for these only, but also for those who believe in me through their word" (John 17:20), he was praying for you and for me.

The Holy Spirit . . . will teach you all things.

—Pat Floyd

A Tongue for Teaching

The Lord God has given me the tongue of a teacher and skill to console the weary with a word.
(Isaiah 50:4 NEB)

Isaiah of Babylon (not Isaiah of the eighth century) was well-educated, a teacher filled with the Spirit of God. Wisdom streamed from his mind and heart and lips—and the harmonies produced by these strands of his being created perhaps the greatest of the prophets. He was at one with the purposes of God. He yearned to help those timid, often suffering servants around him, and through his prophetic ecstasy, God taught him how to sustain with a word those who were weary.

As he carried his message of freedom for his people, he taught his hearers to rethink their view of the Lord God. The Lord, who had vacated Jerusalem in 586 B.C., would return to Jerusalem and lead the captives home. When? Now! And "he will feed his flock like a shepherd, he will gather the lambs in his arms, he will carry them in his bosom, and gently lead those that are with young" (40:11 RSV).

Of those exiles who were tempted to adopt one of the Babylonian deities, Isaiah asked: "To whom then will you liken God, or what likeness compare with him? The idol! a workman casts it, and a goldsmith overlays it with gold (40:18-19). He challenged them: "Lift up your eyes on high and see: who created [the stars]? . . . Have you not known? Have you not heard? The Lord is the everlasting God, the Creator of the ends of the earth" (40:26, 28).

In good professorial style he asks them to think about gods and God: Bel and Nebo are man-made. They cannot move, but are carried as burdens on weary beasts. But who carries the Lord? Ah, he carries you! He tells them to remember the covenants of old: "For I am God, and there is no other; I am God, and there is none like me" (46:9). How much more the educator taught his students is open to those who would like to read!

Blessed are the teachers who know and love God, for God shall give them the tongue of a teacher, that they might lift with words those who are weary.

—*Horace R. Weaver*

The Spiritual Gift

Do not neglect the spiritual gift that is in you.
(I Timothy 4:14a GNB)

Gifts often make me uncomfortable.

It doesn't bother me to give gifts. I like thinking about a person and selecting something special. I enjoy watching a friend's face as she opens a gift from me. Sure, I sometimes worry about whether the gift will be something my friend will enjoy, but that, too, is part of giving. I try to select gifts carefully, thinking about a friend's interests, talents, and concerns. Sometimes I select a gift my friend never would have chosen for himself, but something I see that suits him. Gift giving is fun!

Receiving gifts, however, is another matter. I look at a wrapped gift and frantically try to figure out what it might be. I fix my face in its "ready to smile" pose so my reaction will please the giver. I try to think up thank-yous that are original and reflect the same care that was evidenced in the giving of the gift.

Sometimes the hardest part is using those gifts that were so carefully selected. I look at books I have not taken time to read. I gaze longingly at my wok and wonder if I'll ever take time to learn to use it. I place the shirt I really wanted on a shelf and forget it's there.

Do I do the same with the gifts God has given me? I truly believe God has gifted me with an ability to teach. I love and appreciate children. I enjoy watching and talking and playing with them as they explore God's world. I am enthusiastic about telling stories and will lead any group in singing, if they don't mind a wandering tune.

But do I really nurture this gift? What would it mean to "not neglect" it? Even when I feel incapable of teaching, I know I am still gifted by others in the class. I grow and stretch spiritually as we question, and learn, and play together.

Sometimes my gift remains unused because I need time to stretch and grow. Do I take that time, or merely use this as an excuse to put my gift on the shelf?

Are my thanks-yous to God as carefully thought through as my thank-yous to friends? Can each day be a reminder of the richness of God's gifts? Please, God, let it be so.

And God Gave Gifts

Surely you don't mean me, God.
Are you sure you want to give this gift to me?
I'm truly honored,
But I wonder . . .
My intentions are good,
But my actions don't always follow.
I may intend to use this gift—
But what if I don't?
What if it sits unused?
What if I don't have the time?
What if it isn't quite what I expected?
Help me, God, to accept the What ifs
With a Yes and a Thanks.

—*Mary Jane Pierce Norton*

Take Heed . . . to Your Teaching

Take heed to yourself and to your teaching . . .
for by so doing you will save both yourself
and your hearers.

(I Timothy 4:16 RSV)

In a Thanksgiving Day sermon, Bishop Frank L. Robertson invited us to exercise our gratitude in specific deeds. He suggested that we might seek out a teacher who had been highly influential in our early development but toward whom we had not directed any thought or contact for many years. Then we should call that person, in whatever distant location, and express our indebtedness and gratitude.

For a moment, exercise your own memory to recapture the images of teachers who made a difference in your life — think of one who influenced you far more than you were aware of at the time. In this process you will probably make a discovery: You may be embarrassed to realize that you recall very little of that person's specific words, but very much about his or her attitudes and life-style. You were influenced as much or more by what that teacher was like as by what was said.

First Timothy is a letter of pastoral counsel from an experienced servant of Christ to a young disciple. The writer wants this young colleague to know certain important things early in the pilgrimage. At the heart of the admonitions is this: You teach by what you are as much as by what you say!

The writer calls upon the reader to establish a bifocal view in the teaching role. Through one lens, examine the quality of the data you have to present; through the other lens, examine the quality of life you have to share. The intention of this bifocal view is that the teacher be not judgmental, but therapeutic.

As we teach, we do not come as the wise to the unwise or as the righteous to the unrighteous. Instead, we must approach our calling as those who have seen light and tasted grace, and now want to offer light and share grace. To do so, we must trim the wick of our knowledge while deepening the genuineness of our Christian doing and caring. In teaching, we first teach ourselves; then we become the lesson.

Thus teaching should lead to our own redemption, as well as that of others. Teaching from the mind and heart both stretches the mind and changes the heart. Thereby we do indeed save ourselves—and our hearers.

—Orion N. Hutchinson, Jr.

Teach . . . in All Wisdom

Let the word of Christ dwell in you richly,
teach and admonish one another in all wisdom.
(Colossians 3:16 RSV)

Let the Word of Christ permeate your life, infect your life, become so integrated into your being that your thoughts and actions become synonymous with that Word.

Only then can true praise of God follow—spontaneously, naturally, automatically. Only then can psalms and hymns and spiritual songs be lifted unto the Lord. Only then can we teach and admonish one another in love and joy and Christian fellowship.

And we can do this not because we are worthy, but simply because we are not worthy. We have given God our very unworthiness, and our God has transformed that unworthiness into joy and hope and fulfillment.

That's what happens when we let the Word of Christ dwell in us richly—not only in our thoughts and in our minds, but in our hearts and souls and spirits and actions as well.

Can we teach without the Word of Christ dwelling within us? Perhaps we can. But our teaching under such circumstances is only *about* faith, not the teaching *of* faith. It is teaching about a relationship with the Lord and Master Jesus Christ, not a proclamation of the presence of the Lord Jesus Christ in our lives. It is, to use the common expression, a pooling of ignorance, rather than the joyful song of one beggar telling another where he has discovered bread—the everlasting bread that fulfills all hunger and thirst and loneliness and incompleteness.

So we can teach and admonish if our hearts are filled with Christ. And our teaching and admonishing are not judgmental, pedantic activities, but spring from hearts filled with thanksgiving that sings a song of joy, a psalm of praise, a hymn of wholeness, in and through which those we seek to teach and admonish will catch the wonderful Spirit of God's presence and power.

Let the Word of Christ dwell in you richly. Saturate yourself with that Word. That is the only key to teaching, the only key to learning, the only key to life itself.

—*Jack Gilbert*

He Will Teach Us His Ways

Come, and let us go up to the mountain of the
LORD *. . . and he will teach us of his ways,*
and we will walk in his paths.

(Micah 4:2 KJV)

I remember walking up the mountainside in one of
the largest "favelas," or ghetto areas, in Rio de
Janeiro, Brazil. The path was steep and crumbly; stag-
nant water lay around its edges. A shack with a cross
outside—the church—was our ultimate destination.
What was in this journey for me? What could the
people who lived on this mountain and worshiped in
this ramshackle hut teach me?

The people of this prophecy in Micah will know
what the mountain holds for them. Mountains often
are associated with retreat and reflection. When we
get away from the hustle and bustle of everyday life,
we often find our ears and eyes opened to new meanings.

It is the same for the people who will approach the
mountain in this passage of Scripture. It will be a
popular place: People will "flow" to the mountain of
the house of the Lord. They will come to learn both
new things and a new way of life, to be among people
from other cultures to share, to work toward unity.

This passage gives us deep insight in what we, as
teachers, can offer. We can offer the possibility of new
directions when people encounter us. People of all
nationalities and cultures can have the opportunity

to mingle, swap stories, share customs, think together about mutual concerns. Do we provide opportunities for similar exchanges in our classrooms?

The Scripture reminds us that people will come to the mountain not only to learn of God's ways but to "walk in his paths." When people encounter the mountain they will be educated for change. There will be a change in their spiritual and social directions. Even their economic perspectives will change. They will sit under their own fig trees and vines, and everyone will live an abundant and fruitful life.

Most important, when people come to the mountain they will be educated for peace. We tend to forget that war is learned in much of our culture. We may find it difficult to turn Rambo toys into peaceful alternatives, yet I believe we can teach our children peace amidst war toys and war movies. Our task is to find new ways to resolve conflict and find new meanings for old weapons.

What a legacy we have — to be role models and trail blazers, to show the potential of a new life in Christ Jesus. May people flow to us, and may we teach the ways of Christ, so people can walk with us in the paths of God.

> Lord, let me be your mountain —
>   not that I be personally exalted, no —
> but that others will see me for what I want to be
>   caring, not cold
>   hearing, not hardhearted
>   sensitive, not self-centered;

let these qualities, in me, be exalted,
that others may learn your ways
and walk in them all the days of their life.
"Come, and let us go up to the mountain of the LORD."

— *Faye Wilson-Beach*

PRAYERS

On the First Day of School

Today is the first day, Lord.
I'm excited, but I'm scared, too.
Do you remember the day during my student teaching
    when one of the children talked back? What if that
    happens again? Will I be able to stay calm, to keep
    my own voice steady and kind? I hope so,
    but I'm not sure.
Do you remember how hard I had to work to pass
    math? What if I can't work a problem or answer a
    question? Will I be able to admit my own weakness
    and ask for the help I need?
Do you remember how I almost quit after the first
    month of student teaching? I really do like teaching,
    but the responsibility is so great sometimes.
Will you nudge me when my temper starts to flare?
    when I feel inadequate?
    when I feel overwhelmed?
I can't do this by myself, Lord, but if you'll stay with
    me, I will try. Amen.

—*Gloria V. Thomas*

About Second Thoughts

Dear God, why did I ever agree to teach, feeling so inadequate and lacking in knowledge and skill? Why was I even asked to teach?

The answer: I was willing. Maybe that is all it takes—willingness. I responded to the call to teach as I respond to any task my church asks me to do. I said, "Yes, I'll try." Now I must do as I always have done, go forth on faith—faith that you will provide the knowledge, wisdom, and ability for the task.

I'm no expert at teaching. I do not even know where to start. I'm counting on you, God, to show me the way. Ignite in my heart and mind the light of discovery contained within each lesson, so that I may be able to see your message clearly. Make me your vessel to carry that message to your children.

You know, God, I'm actually excited now, and not quite as afraid. Keep me excited! Stay ever so close to me. Together, we will do O.K.

Oh, yes, one more thing. Thanks for this opportunity to learn more about you through the teachings of your Word. Teach me, Lord, that I may teach. Amen.

—Ellen S. Harkey

About the Vocation of Teaching

Thank you, Master Teacher,
for good role models;
for their inspiration
and tacit lessons
of strength and courage.
Thank you for words spoken
in wisdom and gentleness;
for parents and other teachers
who let me know
there is no nobler calling.
How blessed is the relationship
between teacher and student,
Lord, for in truth,
both teacher and student
are both and the other:
This student is now a teacher,
but this teacher always will be
a student.
Thank you for the call to teach
and to learn.
Amen.

— Patricia Ann Meyers

For Seeing Students as Individuals

Dear God, thank you for allowing me to be in ministry with people. You have called me to teach, Lord, and I want to see each of my students as a gift from you. Each one comes to me in a different wrapping. Some are wrapped beautifully; some look very ordinary; others have been mishandled. Some come very loosely wrapped; others very tightly and every now and then there is a Special Delivery!

But I know the wrapping is not the gift! What is left when the wrapping has been removed is the true gift. Sometimes the package is very easy to open; sometimes I need the help of others. Perhaps some have been opened and the gifts thrown away! And could it be that certain gifts are not for me?

Whatever the wrapping, God, help me always to remember that my students are gifts — gifts received and gifts given, like your Son. Guide me, so that I open each student carefully and see each one as an individual. My response must be one of love and care, just as your Son Christ loves and cares for me.

I pray all this in your name. Amen.

—Lois M. Runk

For Insight

God,
One who knows me
better than I know myself . . .
and loves me with a steadfast love . . .
lead me this day to know you better.
Surprise me with new insights into your activity
in the world, so my students may know you as a God
who is involved in the world—
and in their world. Amen.

—Anonymous

For Effectiveness

Teach me your ways, Lord,
so that I may teach
with love,
with patience,
and with the knowledge
of your presence. Amen.

—Anonymous

About a New Creation

God, I find you making of me a New Creation
—do your creating within me . . .
              through me . . .
              in spite of me.

I give you my preparation time:
—even when I don't know you are preparing me,
—even when I feel I'm experiencing interruptions to
  my preparing,
—especially when I'm struggling for
  creative approaches . . .
  ways to really communicate . . .
  acceptance of my ideas . . .
  completion by a deadline.

God, I find you making of me a New Creation
—and I liked the Old One . . .
—and I felt secure in the Old Place . . .
—and I knew what the Old System expected . . .
  but You are making of me a New Creation.

God, it's painful-joyful . . .
God, it's intense-confusing . . .
God, it's risky-exhilarating . . .
—this creating.

Keep me moving like Sarai . . .
Keep me positioned like Esther . . .
Keep me cooperating like Mary . . .
Keep me carried
  by eagle wings . . .

67

Keep me secured within your Rock . . .
   (though it may be volcanic?)
Keep me walking
   on the path that is
   straightening out ahead of me,
Keep me shaped by Your potter's hands.

God, you gave me birth,
   keep me borning,
   keep me birthing,
   keep creating . . .

Do your incarnating in me . . .
   through me . . .

Till I am finished . . .
Till You are finished!

                    —*Carolyn Hardin Engelhardt*

About Questions and Answers

Dear God, there are so many questions as the children leave the room today.

Have they had a good day?
Will Susan have any supper tonight — or breakfast
  tomorrow?
What should I do about my concern over the hours she
  spends alone?
Has Mike's father returned home — why is he so quiet?
Why won't Gerri ever be quiet?
What kind of day has my son had —
   does his teacher realize that
   though he doesn't express his thoughts well
     in words,
   he expresses himself in his drawing?
What will we have for supper?
Have the children seen Christ in me today?

So many questions as the children leave.

Help me remember, God, that the answer to all the questions is you and my personal experience of you. It is your indwelling presence in me that can help me understand the answers. It is the certainty of your ever-present Spirit that helps me understand, too, that the questions I cannot put into words can be answered. Guide me through each day; give me the wisdom to ask the questions I feel and the courage to follow where your answers lead. In the name of the indwelling Christ, I pray. Amen.

—Martha W. Hazzard

For Being True to God's Purposes

It's the "Greatest Story Ever Told."
It's part of who I am.
It's "totally awesome"
   to think about teaching someone else.
It's so personal,
    so universal,
    so profound,
    so simple.
Lord, help me remember that I am teaching students,
   not curriculum, and that all I need to teach,
   you have already given me.

It doesn't matter how fancy the classroom is, how
   many students there are, or that I am more scared
   of my students than they are of me. What really
   matters is You.
And I know You will be present with all of us,
   no matter what.

Thank you, Lord, for the privilege of teaching.
Calm my anxious heart.
   Teach me, Lord, that I may teach,
   and we will all grow in
   knowledge and grace. Amen.

—Patricia Ann Meyers

For Sensitivity to Students' Needs

So it is true. Jimmy's parents have separated. This may explain why Jimmy has missed several times, and why, when he is here, he is distant. I scolded him the other day, Lord. I wish I hadn't. I realize now that what was in his eyes was hurt.

Heavenly Father, I sense some hurt, too, in my own heart. Everything has been going so well — no serious problems in class, compliments from several other teachers — but I think I have missed some things. I suspect there are several Jimmys. I can remember when I was much more concerned about this class than I have been recently. I remember when I prayed each day that I would be a witness for Christ, and I've neglected that. I have been thinking much more about my own ability than about thanking you for the gift you have given me to teach.

Cleanse me, Lord, in the name of Jesus. Trouble me when I need to be troubled, and help me to feel the pain of others, even as you felt my pain on Calvary's cross. Amen.

—Riley B. Case

For Students from Unhappy Homes

O God, I see so much unhappiness among my students. On the surface they seem to have so much, especially things. But yet they feel they do not have enough to be happy. Here are unhappy people from unhappy homes. Help me to help them.

I'm not so sure I want to help them find happiness in the customary sense. To me, happiness is a by-product of something that is much more enduring. Help me to instill in each student a sense of self-worth, an incomparable value given them at birth. For each is born in your image, each given a portion of the Divine. Help me whisper your secret in their ears — that happiness will come when they find the way to unleash your Spirit within themselves, to be all they can be and serve you by serving others, using your Son as the perfect example of a true offspring of God.

I confess I'm asking for true happiness for each member of your family — including me. I, too, need to be reminded from time to time that you, loving Father, are the source of all happiness! Amen.

—Ellen S. Harkey

For the Child Who Needs Extra Love

Dear God, Tommy is Your child, too.
So why can't I love him as I love the others?
There are times when I see a hungry look in his eyes,
That lost look;
That look that says he wants so desperately
To be loved and appreciated.
But most of the time, dear God,
You know he comes into the room like a whirlwind,
Loud, and disruptive, and inconsiderate of others.
Most of the time I can give him special attention
And direct his boundless energy into a creative task.

But yesterday — Oh, yesterday
When he ran his black marker in squiggles
All over the Valentine bulletin board that
Jamie and Anne had worked so hard to decorate for
    our party,
I'm afraid I forgot all about positive reinforcement,
And ignoring negative behavior, and all those
Good modeling techniques I had learned to practice.
In a word, I blew up, and the whole class saw
That other side of me.
Forgive me, dear God,
Help the children to forgive me,
And help me to forgive myself, and to grow through
This experience,
And to learn to show my love to Tommy
Even as You would have me love this special child of
    Yours!

                                    — Helen Monroe

For Patience in Meetings

Dear God,
Sitting in meetings is so time-consuming,
So tiring, so uninspiring . . .
And are we really getting anywhere?
I do try to listen,
To hear the frustration and the pain,
The questions and the struggles of others.

Help us to keep on track —
To keep the vision of the goals we set,
To hear Your voice and be sensitive to Your will,
Even as we continue searching for solutions.

And dear God,
When there must be conflicts of ideas —
And there must, since we are all so different —
Help us to disagree in love,
To be able to see the big picture,
To compromise our petty desires for
The good of all concerned.
Help us to look beyond today, this month, this year,
And take a longer view to the ultimate goal
For our work here.

—Helen Monroe

About Endings and Beginnings

O eternal God of our past, our present, and our future, I come to you as I come to the end of a period and a task, and must begin anew. Endings leave us often frustrated, or even haunted. Beginnings can make us fearful.

You are both the eternal truth and the etenal I AM. You are with us where we are, to offer us what we need to know and to be. You can be our bridge of sustenance and hope over the surging stream of change. Save me from being so shackled by what has been that I cannot enter with eagerness into what can be. May I be enabled to find both lasting benediction in what has ended and blessed satisfaction in what is beginning.

One thing I would seek and do, Divine Enabler. Even "forgetting what is behind me and reaching out for that which lies ahead," enable me thereby to "press towards the goal to win the prize, which is God's call to the life above in Christ Jesus" (Phil. 3:13b-14 GNB).

> Through this changing world below,
> Lead me gently, gently as I go;
> Trusting thee, I cannot stray;
> I can never, never lose my way.
> *(Fanny J. Crosby)*

Amen.

—*Orion N. Hutchinson, Jr.*

At the Beginning of a New School Year

All-knowing God, the dawn of another year is here.
Hear me, I pray, as I reflect on the teaching ministry
you have called me to do:

For strength to bear
    the task so clear,
    I pray be near.

For guidance and direction for the road ahead,
    Your wisdom I covet
    Help me ne'er forget.

For insights and challenges brought,
    By lessons taught,
    Your Spirit sought.

For love you share
    because you care,
    My lesson plans I prepare.

For joy and peace
    You alone can give,
    I humbly seek.

For solitude and calm
    When trials come,
    Grant me the Gilead balm. Amen.

—MarLu Primero Scott

After an Especially Difficult Day

O Thou who hast said unto us that we "shall mount up with wings as eagles . . . run, and not be weary . . . walk, and not faint" (Isa. 40:31 KJV), I confess that this evening I feel more like a wingless bird, a weary jogger, or a fainting hiker. The demands of the day have drained my resources, and the frustrations of the hours have left me with a sense of futility. I would like the consolation of thinking that I'm "weary with well-doing," but I even doubt that the doing was all that well.

Have mercy upon me, O God. It was to those who "wait upon the Lord" that these energizing gifts were promised. So I would wait upon Thee now.

Spirit consoling, let us find
   Thy hand when sorrows leave us blind;
In the gray valley let us hear
   Thy silent voice, "Lo, I am near."
Spirit of love, at evening time
   When weary feet refuse to climb,
Give us thy vision, eyes that see,
   Beyond the dark, the dawn, and Thee.
                 (Earl Marlatt)

Indeed, lift my eyes beyond these shadows of earth so that I may see anew the light of thine eternal compassion and power. So shall my strength be renewed in a new way for a new day.

For Christ's sake, and mine. Amen.

—Orion N. Hutchinson, Jr.

For Renewal

In the quietness of this moment, O God,
I wait upon you.

For you have promised renewed strength to those
 who wait.
And, O Lord, you know that I need my strength
 renewed.
I am worn out, and my patience is threadbare.

But I hold tight to your promises:
That I should mount up with wings as eagles
That I should run and not be weary
That I should walk and not faint.

There was a time when I only wanted to mount up
with wings as eagles. And if I couldn't do that,
at least run and not be weary.

Today, Lord, I trust in you for my help, and I'm willing to
just walk, if need be, but let me go forward
 in Thy name. Amen.

—Haviland C. Houston

For a New Birth

Dear God, I am so tired. Maybe I've been at this job of teaching too long. What started out as fun, challenging, and exciting has turned into just a job. What has happened? Where has the excitement gone?

Divine helper, I'm asking for a conversion, a turnaround, a new birth. I am asking for the resurrection of a teaching spirit within me. But, please, let this resurrection take three days to come about. Right now I need a time of peace and quiet, of rest and nourishment. In three days I should be ready to try my wings again.

I turn to you for strength, for I know you are the source of all power. Ignite in me a spark of enthusiasm for the task at hand. Help me to find a new challenge, a new perspective, a new desire for growth. As I see it, if I cannot find something new to learn, then that which I teach will be tiresome and repetitious.

I'm so glad you are here for me. Thanks for listening, my God-friend. Thanks for working another of your miracles in my life. Amen.

—Ellen S. Harkey

For Humility

O God, I come to you this morning low in spirit—
    I didn't have a good day yesterday;
      Two of the class members engaged in an angry
        dispute that didn't seem to have much to do
        with Christian living and faith;
      I have spent so many hours planning and
        preparing for the workshop to train teachers
       —they need it so much!
      But I cannot find enough
      who are willing to attend to have it—
I am so tired, I work for so many hours every week,
      I plan, I study, I prepare to teach and to lead,
      I try to challenge others—
    But after a day like yesterday I am tired and
      discouraged.
    I wonder why I keep working at this job—
I truly do try to work for *your* honor and glory, Lord,
    But I guess sometimes my *self* gets in the way.
Forgive me, Lord—
    Strengthen me,
    Sustain me,
    Help me to remember that all you require of me is
      faithful service—
    That you are there to support me in all I do, if it is
      done according to *your* will, not mine. Amen.

—Esther L. Megill

About Grace and Teaching and Learning

It is humbling, God,
to know that
my students are learning
whether I am teaching them or not.
It is awe-inspiring, Lord,
to think that
education takes place
in the relationship
between teacher and student.
There are so many variables in a classroom:
Each student's hidden agenda;
Each one's cognitive, emotional, and physical
        development;
    Texts, vocabulary, energy levels —
all so different.
When I stop to think about it,
that real education takes place is a miracle . . .
Except for that other variable —
Grace.
By your grace, this teacher teaches and learns.
By your grace, the student learns and teaches.
Thank you
for grace,
    courage,
        wisdom;
For students,
And for the privilege of being a part of the exciting
    enterprise of education. Amen.

—*Patricia Ann Meyers*

For Ability to Make Faith Contagious

What do I want to accomplish by my teaching, O Lord?

Serve my church? Yes—but there are other ways I could serve. Why did I choose to serve this way?

To do my part? Yes—but what is my part? When I've done all, I'm still an unprofitable servant.

To transmit facts? Yes—but I confess my limited knowledge. I didn't agree to teach because I had all the answers.

I think that down deep, something or Someone came to me once upon a time. Although it brought an awareness of sin, it also brought an experience of grace. I found a sense of worth and purpose, and your resources for my life. I found a caring for others which leaped over barriers. At times unaware, sometimes very aware, my life has arisen out of those discoveries, imperfectly but definitely. Through your revelations through persons, I found my magnificent obsession.

Why do I teach? I think I've just discovered why! Out of your grace, you brought me the best of my life and being. And it came, gratefully, through persons as human as I am.

O dear Enabler, now I would be one of those persons for someone else. May my teaching be the sharing of not just what I know, but what I've found—truly a treasure hidden in our fields, in the manner of Jesus, who made faith contagious. Amen.

—*Orion N. Hutchinson, Jr.*

For a Little More Assertiveness

Dear God,
Why is it so hard for me to pick up the phone
And ask a friend to help me with a job?
Why do I put off this task until it is
Almost too late, and everyone is involved
With other work?

Visiting with a friend in her home
Is one of the pleasures I enjoy most.
And almost always, that friend is willing
To consider and pray about a position
For which she is so well qualified.

So why do I delay asking a friend
To help teach boys and girls in our church?
Help me find the right moment, the right words,
And the most attractive job to match the gifts
For each of your servants in our congregation.

And, dear God, don't let me forget to ask You
To come with me when I do the asking! Amen.

—*Helen Monroe*

For Patience

Loving God, here I am again, wanting answers, results, and quick fixes. I keep running but getting nowhere. Help me to slow down. Help me take the time to breathe in the reality of your presence in my life. Help me to listen and, most of all, really hear what you are saying to me. When I only admit that all it takes is openness to you, all my inadequacies do fade away. I can take time to "smell the roses" and, at the same time, have all the strength and energy I so desperately seek. When I hear what you are saying, I can concentrate on the tasks that lie before me.

God of all life, I ask for your continuing patience with me—I do so desperately need it. Grant the serenity that comes from hearing what you are saying and the life that comes when I finally respond to your word. I ask all this in the name of Jesus the Christ. Amen.

—Martha Stoneburner

For Conviction Amidst Personal Doubt

O Spirit of truth, the more I study and learn, the more I question and doubt. Help me realize that this is not bad, because questioning and doubting are part of maturing — going on to perfection. May I not feel it necessary to blindly accept beliefs handed me by others, but feel a freedom to explore for myself, to find what I truly believe. True religion is such a personal thing. So many seem to believe so easily. But to make a conviction uniquely my own, I must reach it through my own personal faith-journey. Lord, "I believe; help my unbelief!" (Mark 9:24 RSV)

While struggling to believe, I recall with thanks the guidance I received on my journey from those farther along the way, those who have so led me to truth that it has become my own. May I be that kind of person for others — not limiting their beliefs by forcing on them my own or boxing them in through my lack of knowledge or understanding of truth.

Let me be a lamplighter, illuminating the way for my students to find your truths for themselves, while I am doing the same, led by your Spirit. Amen.

—Ellen S. Harkey

For Help in Dealing with Roadblocks

Dear God,
How can I face this one more obstacle?
Just when I thought all the plans were in order,
When the whole design team seemed to be on board
And we were about to go into action,
Then we discovered the money for this project
Had been given to another group.

Forgive me, dear God,
Please, I don't want to be jealous;
I know their ministry is important, too,
But how shall I go to those who have worked so hard
And tell them our plans will also have to include
Where the money may be found?
It just isn't fair!

Please, God, help us find the way
You would want us to go.
We know that if a door closes
You can be depended upon to open a window.
Help us find that window, dear God,
Before we become so discouraged we lose heart.
Show us the way
And give us the strength to go on!

—*Helen Monroe*

For Attention to Tasks

Dear God, You know me.
You know me better than I know myself.
And yet You still love me.
Thank You, God.

You know I am a procrastinator —
I put things off until the dread of them
Overwhelms me.
Not big jobs to begin with,
But little bothersome routine tasks,
Which hang over me undone
Until they take on monstrous proportions —
At least in my mind.

Like straightening my desk
Or cleaning closets;
Giving away unused clothing
Or clearing files of needless paper;
Or designing my teaching a whole year ahead,
Getting the big picture solidly in mind.

Forgive me, dear God.
Thank You for your infinite patience with me.
Give me the strength and courage to do
One job at a time, completing it;
Taking one day at a time, enjoying to the fullest,
And doing my best with each one.

—Helen Monroe

About Feeling Unequal to the Task

The Teacher

Lord, who am I to teach the way
To little children day by day,
So prone myself to go astray?

I teach them *knowledge,* but I know
How faint they flicker and how low
The candles of my knowledge glow.

I teach them *power* to will and do,
But only now to learn anew
My own great weakness through
   and through.

I teach them *love* for all mankind
And all God's creatures, but I find
My love comes lagging far behind.

Lord, if their guide I still must be
Oh, let the little children see
The teacher leaning hard on Thee.

—*Leslie Pinckney Hill*

For Peace

How can I bring Peace to my world —
Even to my small community —
When I am not at peace with myself?
Forgive me, God, for setting
Unrealistic goals for myself,
For taking on too many jobs,
For trying to carry the burdens of others
And asking too much of myself.
Forgive me for being impatient.
Help me to stop, dear God,
To listen for your voice,
To gain strength from fellowship with You,
To rest quietly in Your care
So that I may serve You more fully,
That I may enjoy and appreciate
Your children more
And that my room, my little world,
May become an island of Peace,
A place of repose for the weary,
A source of joy for the disconsolate,
A well of love for the lonely,
And a core of strength for the weak.
Thank You, dear God,
For promising peace
beyond our understanding.
Help us search until we find that Peace.

—Helen Monroe

Before Chaperoning a Trip

Eternal God,
As we board our transportation
We ask for a safe journey.
Give us alert and careful drivers.
Help us to establish and strengthen friendships
during this trip.
May the relationship between youths and adults
grow stronger.
Give the adults listening hearts
That will not miss opportunities to guide
in loving ways.
Bring us home wiser, more loving,
Closer in our relationship with *you*,
And all in one piece!
Amen.

—*Geneala V. Swink*

For Students During Examination Time

Most merciful God, creator of the human mind, I come to you today for special blessings on my students who are taking exams. Please give them clarity of mind and empty them of confusing thoughts. Help them remember past learnings and insights that will free them to respond to the questions. Forgive those times when relying on one's own ability seems the right thing to do. Grant them courage to face whatever results the exams will unfold. Restore their confidence when their expectations do not match the exam results. Reassure them that you are ever present, through laurels or Waterloos. All this I ask in the name of Jesus, the Master Teacher. Amen.

—MarLu Primero Scott

After a Frustrating Day

Lord, your ways are truly the ways of love, hope, and joy. I confess I don't always feel loving, especially when my class does not seem to respond. I know it may be my lack of preparation with you as I study. It may have been an "off" day with the students. If I let you down, or the students, please forgive me. I am thankful that you are present at all times, even in the difficult times. A lesson can be learned through it all. I offer you my time, for preparation; myself, as an instrument of your love, so my students may discover you anew in each situation in life. Amen.

—Anonymous

At the End of the Year

The New Leaf

He came to my desk with quivering lip —
    The lesson was done.
"Dear Teacher, I want a new leaf," he said,
    "I have spoiled this one."
I took the old leaf, stained and blotted,
And gave him a new one, all unspotted,
    And into his sad eyes smiled:
    "Do better now, my child!"

I went to the Throne with a quivering soul —
    The old year was done.
"Dear Father, hast Thou a new leaf for me?
    "I have spoiled this one."
He took the old leaf, stained and blotted,
And gave me a new one, all unspotted,
    And into my sad heart smiled:
    "Do better now, my child!"

—*Author Unknown*